There is nothing more important in a world gone wrong than to help children, young people, and adults develop and live by a biblical worldview. We need to hear from seasoned individuals who have lived life to the full and discovered the eternal value of living by the Word of God at every turn and stage of life. I have personally known Warren since I was a boy and have watched him face his own challenges of singleness, parenting, working, grandparenting, and retirement. This booklet is steeped in his deep commitment to God, his family, and his fellow man over many years. You won't go wrong by taking someone else through the insights and wise advice of this guide for life.

—Rev. Ken Ingram
Church Care Pastor
West Highland Baptist Church of Hamilton, Ontario

17 Guides in Life for Adults of All
Ages to Live Their Best Life

Guidance for Life

Warren Lemon

GUIDANCE FOR LIFE
Copyright © 2024 by Warren Lemon

All rights reserved. Neither this publication nor any part of this publication may be reproduced or transmitted in any form or by any means, electronic or mechanical, including photocopying, recording or any information storage and retrieval system, without permission in writing from the author.

Scriptures taken from the Holy Bible, New International Version®, NIV®. Copyright © 1973, 1978, 1984, 2011 by Biblica, Inc.™ Used by permission of Zondervan. All rights reserved worldwide. www.zondervan.com The "NIV" and "New International Version" are trademarks registered in the United States Patent and Trademark Office by Biblica, Inc.™

ISBN: 978-1-4866-2571-0
eBook ISBN: 978-1-4866-2572-7

Word Alive Press
119 De Baets Street Winnipeg, MB R2J 3R9
www.wordalivepress.ca

Cataloguing in Publication information can be obtained from Library and Archives Canada.

CONTENTS

1: THE MOST IMPORTANT QUESTION ANYONE CAN ASK: "WHAT MUST I DO TO BE SAVED?" ... 1

2: GET THIS RIGHT! ... 4

3: LEARN FROM THE ANT ... 7

4: CHOOSE YOUR CLOSEST FRIENDS WISELY ... 10

5: THE NEED FOR PRAYER ... 13

6: AVOID ALL FORMS OF GAMBLING, LOTTERIES, AND GET RICH SCHEMES ... 16

7: PERSISTENCE AND DETERMINATION ... 18

8: BUILD SOLID RELATIONSHIPS WITH YOUR FAMILY AND COMMUNITY ... 22

9: DISPLAY STRENGTH AND COURAGE ... 25

10: WHAT THE BIBLE SAYS ABOUT MONEY AND STEWARDSHIP ... 27

11: CHRISTIAN CAMPING AND MISSION TRIPS ... 31

12: SUDBURY VISIT OF CROSSES ... 34

13: WHEN MEDITATING ON A BIBLE PASSAGE ... 36

14: GIVE THANKS FOR THE HARD TIMES ... 38

15: MAKE WISE CHOICES THAT WILL MAKE YOUR PARENTS PROUD ... 40

16: A TWELVE-POINT EXHORTATION FOR ALL ... 43

17: CREATE OR DO SOMETHING THAT WILL BE OF LASTING VALUE TO YOURSELF AND OTHERS ... 45

ABOUT THE AUTHOR ... 51

1
THE MOST IMPORTANT QUESTION ANYONE CAN ASK: "WHAT MUST I DO TO BE SAVED?"

WHEN I WAS growing up in New Brunswick, I didn't fully realize or understand how God was working in my life to eventually bring me to salvation. When I went to Ontario in 1963 at the age of nineteen, I had an emptiness inside me, a vacuum, which I know now was the convicting power of the Holy Spirit. The Holy Spirit kept me free of a host of issues which could have altered my life in a very negative direction.

I heard the gospel call in Kapuskasing while regularly attending the Kapuskasing Baptist Church and responded to the invitation for salvation in March 1966. The emptiness I'd had within me for years went away, and it has never returned. What I craved wasn't *something* but rather *someone*. And that someone was Jesus.

> Believe in the Lord Jesus, and you will be saved… (Acts16:31)

We should never underestimate the influence of God's Word to convict and save lives. Over my lifetime, I have personally observed hundreds of lives transformed through the power of the Holy Spirit. The faithful work of Christian organizations, churches, personal witnesses, and the placement of Bibles does produce results.

> Show us your unfailing love, Lord, and grant
> us your salvation. (Psalm 85:7)

When my wife Evelyn was a young girl at the age of five in New Liskeard in 1953, a concerned neighbour asked her mother if she could take Evelyn to Sunday school and church. Her mother wisely agreed and Evelyn gave her heart to the Lord at a young age. She has been faithful ever since. Her first pastor referred to Evelyn as "one of the Lord's shining lights." Such is the power and reward of the personal invitation to come and see.

Evelyn Dunbrack as a five-year-old in the first grade.

God's Word instructs us to be on guard against deceptive worldly philosophy rather than focusing on Christ.

> See to it that no one takes you captive through hollow and deceptive philosophy, which depends on human tradition and the elemental spiritual forces of this world rather than on Christ. (Colossians 2:8)

2
GET THIS RIGHT!

FOR YOUR MARRIAGE partner of the opposite sex, make the right choice. I once saw a wall plaque with a quote from author H. Jackson Brown. On that plaque, he laid out his twenty-one suggestions for success in life. This was his first suggestion: "Marry the right person. This one decision will determine 90% of your happiness or misery." I tell this to every young person I can. Virtually everyone agrees, especially older married adults.

On a trip to Israel in 2017, our group was at the airport in Tel Aviv awaiting our plane for the return trip to Canada. Our tour leader's two unmarried grandsons were standing nearby and I walked up to them.

"Could I give you two young men a word of wisdom from a senior citizen?" I asked as I put my arm around these young men.

They didn't quite know what to think but did agree to it, since their grandparents were there and also wondering what I would say.

"Marry the right person," I stated slowly and emphatically. "This one decision will determine ninety percent of your happiness or misery."

The grandparents agreed that this was sound advice.

I once read in a book the story of a few young women at a Christian college who had a question of concern for their guest speaker. The women said that they'd likely marry at some point, but they wanted to know which quality they should most look for in a future husband.

The speaker thought for a moment and then said, "Teachability. A man who will be led by the Lord and have a teachable spirit."

"There aren't many Christian men like that," one of the women said.

"You only need one."

While standing in line at a coffee shop on January 24, 2023, Evelyn told me that she would grab a seat while I stayed in line to order our drinks. I did so.

Just then, a woman behind me in the line said, "You listen very well."

Yes, I'm teachable.

In church one Sunday in 2022, an excited young woman came up to me with her new husband.

"Mr. Lemon, I took your advice of marrying the right man," she said. "God gave him to me."

She told me later that she had previously been in a youth group where I had shared about the importance of marrying the right person. She had not forgotten that advice.

The couple was baptized in August 2022 and both became regular church attenders.

I've been going to church regularly for fifty-eight years and have made some observations about young men who seek young women in church.

In a few instances, I've seen non-Christian men attend with their Christian girlfriends. Although they eventually marry, a troubling pattern sometimes emerges when the new husband suddenly stops attending church and loses all interest in spiritual matters.

A young woman should be as certain as she can be that she is getting what she wants from her future husband. For that matter, any man or woman should prove their spiritual authenticity by regularly attending church for at least a year before marriage. This should be accompanied by a public profession of their faith through baptism.

Additionally, seek wise counsel from senior Christians about the wisdom of marrying any individual. Nobody wants to marry a wolf in sheep's clothing.

> Do not be yoked together with unbelievers. For what do righteousness and wickedness have in common? Or what fellowship can light have with darkness? (2 Corinthians 6:14)

Before the American wife of author C.S. Lewis died at the age of forty-five in 1960, she turned to her husband and said simply, "You have made me happy." And then she added, "I am at peace with God."[1]

---

[1] Michael Coren, *The Man Who Created Narnia: The Story of C.S. Lewis* (San Francisco, CA: Ignatius Press, 2006), 108.

3
LEARN FROM THE ANT

> Go to the ant, you sluggard; consider its ways and be wise! It has no commander, no overseer or ruler, yet it stores its provisions in summer and gathers its food at harvest. How long will you lie there, you sluggard? When will you get up from your sleep? A little sleep, a little slumber, a little folding of the hands to rest—and poverty will come on you like a thief and scarcity like an armed man. (Proverbs 6:6–11)

MY PARENTS WERE both hard workers. In fact, everybody I knew growing up worked for what they got. My brother and sister were ambitious, too, and I was also. It just didn't feel right not to be busy at something. For example, at the age of nine I would earn money by picking strawberries. I did all types of jobs for contractors and seniors.

When I married in August 1969, I was very motivated to start construction on our new home on some property we had purchased. From the time we excavated the basement to our move-in date, two months passed. The house was far from finished, but by June 1, 1970 we were already paying off our mortgage as opposed to rent.

Evelyn and I worked tirelessly every hour that was available to us. I didn't have to be told to work, as I was a self-starter. I didn't have to be pulled out of my bed. And my wife worked just as faithfully as I did. She supported me fully.

> Nothing gets done if you stay in bed. There is no substitute for good old-fashioned work.[2]
> —John Wooden

> Whatever you do, work at it with all your heart, as working for the Lord, not for human masters… (Colossians 3:23)

For decades, my wife and I have endeavoured to keep our neighbourhood clean by properly disposing of roadside garbage. After I retired in 2004 at the age of sixty, I was approached by two different employers offering me a position to supervise employees. They did this directly because they had observed me regularly doing volunteer work and were impressed with my ambition.

I did accept the first offer of employment and worked all of one winter at a cedar sawmill.

Employers are always seeking individuals who consistently display initiative. Other people have bought coffee and stopped to comment on how they appreciated our cleanup efforts. Evelyn and I have never been too proud to get our hands soiled to tackle the dirtier tasks of life when it's for a common good.

For two and a half years, from 2000 to 2003, I did most of the weekly preaching at our church, as we didn't have a pastor. And I was working full-time during this period. Looking back,

---

[2] John Wooden, *Wooden on Leadership* (New York, NY: McGraw Hill, 2005), 20.

I really don't know how I did it, but God gave me the desire, ability, and mental health to do so.

> Never be lacking in zeal, but keep your spiritual fervor, serving the Lord. (Romans 12:11)

4
CHOOSE YOUR CLOSEST FRIENDS WISELY

MOST MEN DON'T have a lot of male friends. We're blessed if we have at least one close male friend.

My one good friend was a fellow Gideon member, Charles Shouldice. I recruited Charles in 1993, along with his wife. We served together in our churches and in the Share Word Global ministry for twenty-three years before Charles died in a fall in December 2016. We travelled many miles together doing Gideon ministry, attending functions, and meeting locally with other Gideons. We were almost a clone of each other, shared a lot of life, and our individual lives were enriched because of our friendship.

I gave the eulogy at his funeral in Kapuskasing and made reference to an article called "The Gift of a Friend" by Steve Kennedy, the editor of a Christian magazine. In reference to close friends, he wrote, "I've learned to listen for God's voice in the voice of such friends."[3]

When Evelyn and I married in August 1969, life was a bit lonely for Evelyn. I was away most days during the week and Evelyn was new to marriage and living in Kapuskasing. Her

---

[3] Stephen Kennedy, "The Gift of a Friend," *Testimony*. Date of access: March 13, 2024 (https://testimony.paoc.org/editorials/the-gift-of-a-friend).

best friend immediately became Gwen Baker, wife of the pastor at Kapuskasing Baptist Church. Gwen was Evelyn's mentor regarding marriage, as the Bakers had been married ten years at the time. That seemed like a lifetime to Evelyn! Evelyn would often say that even after they hadn't seen each other for years, being with Gwen again always made it feel like they'd never parted.

Youth need to choose their closest friends wisely. We often hear of individuals getting in with the wrong crowd. If that's the case, some friendships may need to be severed and new friendships developed.

I noticed a poster in a mall years ago that had the photo of a young deceased male lying on a slab in a morgue with a string and tag attached to his large toe. Inscribed on the tag were these words: "He really tied one on last night." This poster was delivering an important message about being wise in selecting one's friends, as well as the evils and consequences of alcohol and drug abuse.

> Bad company corrupts good character. (1 Corinthians 15:33)
>
> For lack of guidance a nation falls, but victory is won through many advisers. (Proverbs 11:14)
>
> Whoever heeds life-giving correction will be at home among the wise… but the one who heeds correction gains understanding. (Proverbs 15:31–32)
>
> Walk with the wise and become wise, for a companion of fools suffers harm. (Proverbs 13:20)

The simple truth here is that we become like those we keep company with. Choose your friends with care. Proverbs 2:20 further tells us to *"walk in the ways of good and keep to the paths of the righteous."* A final cautionary verse is found in Proverbs 12:26: *"The righteous choose their friends carefully…"*

Kapuskasing women enjoying bonding time together at a weekend conference on June 2–4, 2006 in Huntsville, Ontario.

5
THE NEED FOR PRAYER

EVELYN AND I pray in our car for safety before setting out on a journey. We also give thanks for the natural beauty we see along the way and the people we meet.

On one occasion in Algonquin Park in September 2018, a large male deer darted quickly across the road in front of our car. It missed us by half a second.

On two other previous occasions, one in the darkness of night and one in full daylight, God held moose either on the centre line or turned them back from crossing a major highway. Both instances had the potential for serious injury, for us as well as the moose.

And we don't know how many other times God has protected us without us even being aware of it.

On yet another instance on a cold -30ºC evening on January 26, 1972, when I was just twenty-eight, I was driving home alone on an icy winter road. I had just finished performing my duties as a foreman in supervising the hauling of four-foot pulpwood from the bush to the mill in Kapuskasing. I approached a narrow single-lane bridge on which I had the right of way. An oncoming truck was returning empty from the mill, making his truck available for the night shift driver in the bush. I realized he wasn't going to stop and I didn't have time to stop before he entered the bridge. I sped up as fast as I could and made it across the bridge with a split second to spare. My young wife was very nearly made a widow that night, just three years into our marriage and with an eight-month-old baby at home. Thank God for her daily prayers for my safety.

Make prayer a vital part of your everyday life and ask for God's protecting hand. Prayer does work.

> The prayer of a righteous man is powerful and effective. (James 5:16)

Another aspect of prayer concerns a church in Kapuskasing where I was a member. The Bridge Bible Church was praying for a permanent facility. A large grocery chain had recently closed and a Christian in another town had influence over who the facility would be sold or donated to. I agreed to be on the board to pray for the sale, or gift, of the building. But as time progressed, it became apparent that God was closing the door to us.

Next we prayed for a suitable house for our pastor and wife, and a vacant home did come up for sale. I attempted to purchase the home, but my numerous low offers were always rejected.

Our church closed in January 2012 because of a number of factors. In hindsight, I was certainly thankful that God had answered our prayers in His wisdom, and not ours in regards to both of these buildings. It would have stressed me greatly to be individually responsible for such a large debt. This would surely have had a negative effect on my health and marriage.

The lesson I learned here is that God has His reasons for not always granting us what we pray for. We may not realize it immediately, but in God's timing we learn that His will for us is best. God does answer prayer one way or another, and we need to ask for His will and for Him to open and close doors.

6
AVOID ALL FORMS OF GAMBLING, LOTTERIES, AND GET RICH SCHEMES

WHEN MY WIFE and I travelled on a cruise ship to Alaska in 2004, all the passengers had to walk through a casino one evening in order to reach a concert. This was a sly tactic to lure gamblers, and possibly new gamblers, to the glimmer and glamour of all types of one-armed bandits.

I made a decision decades ago to never purchase lottery tickets, as it can be too addictive. All too often, the busiest kiosk or store in a mall is the one where lottery tickets of all stripes are sold. And many of the most loyal customers live on fixed incomes; they can least afford to gamble the limited resources they do have.

There was a time in years past when most gambling took the form of bingo. Gambling has advanced now to a thriving and growing industry all over the world. Far too many people are lured by the deceptive lie that they can get rich quick rather than acquiring wealth by working or investing over a lifetime.

Canadians are now bombarded like never before to indulge in all types of addictive gambling. This can ruin a career, marriage, or family. It can even end lives. Don't be misled by the daily advertising seen on television and billboards insinuating that you can become radiantly happy and rich by gambling. Gambling ads on television in Ontario now shamelessly state that they're "bringing Las Vegas to Ontario." Not every gambler is a winner, though, and the odds are definitely not in the gambler's favour.

A former pastor of West Highland Baptist Church in Hamilton, Ontario once wrote an extensive report on gambling titled "A Pastor's Reflection on the Forgotten Factors of Gambling." Copies can be obtained by contacting that church.

Matthew 6:19–21 gives us words of warning and wisdom on storing up treasures in heaven:

> Do not store up for yourselves treasures on earth, where moths and vermin destroy, and where thieves break in and steal. But store up for yourselves treasures in heaven, where moths and vermin do not destroy, and where thieves do not break in and steal. For where your treasure is, there your heart will be also.

The government of Ontario announced on August 29, 2023 that the province would ban the use of athletes in advertising for online gambling, while also strengthening standards to restrict the use of celebrities whom the government says might appeal to minors.

That ban came into effect on February 28, 2024 with the Ontario provincial regulator stating that the move would help safeguard children and youth. Athletes, whether active or retired, are also now banned from participating in ads for Ontario gaming operators.

It's been shown that when people start gambling at an early age, they are more likely to get addicted to gambling. And that is certainly true.

7
PERSISTENCE AND DETERMINATION

PERSISTENCE IS A person's steadfastness to stay the course for the long-term rather than wandering here and there for brief periods. Determination means that you have your mind made up, that you are resolved and unwavering.

Here's a biblical example of being persistent in prayer:

> Then Jesus said to them, "Suppose you have a friend, and you go to him at midnight and say, 'Friend, lend me three loaves of bread; a friend of mine on a journey has come to me, and I have no food to offer him…' because of your shameless audacity he will surely get up and give you as much as you need." (Luke 11:5–6, 8)

A good personal example is that of an individual writing a book. It's so much easier to give up and convince yourself that today's generation doesn't read, that books are expensive to print and your time could be better used elsewhere. You have to be determined to do the best you can and persist—that is, if you feel that God is calling you to record your story for the future benefit of others.

Another excellent example is that of being a fifty-year active member of Share Word Global (the Gideons) and placing or distributing Scriptures for people to read. We don't immediately see results, but we do know that when we're obedient to our calling God will bless our efforts.

When Kimberly Clark announced in 1990 that the paper mill in Kapuskasing, Ontario would be vastly downsized and put up for sale, it was shocking and devastating news for me, as an employee, as well as for the town and the six hundred employees. Rather than accept our fate, though, all were of the general consensus that we should fight to save our town, our mill, our jobs, and our future.

The premier of Ontario, Bob Rae, stepped in to help. A large delegation, including me, travelled to Queen's Park in Toronto to protest. The entire town banded together in common cause.

Kimberly Clark offered to donate the mill to the employees, provided certain conditions were met. To have funds in reserve, $20 million dollars had to be raised by the employees and its citizens. I borrowed $15,000 to purchase shares in the new company, which was named Spruce Falls Inc. A necessary strategic and qualified partner was located in Quebec, and it was called TEMBEC.

On December 3, 1991, the employees took ownership and the mill was saved. This was the largest buyout of a company in Ontario's history. It mainly happened because of the determination and persistence of many.

In 1964, while I was living in Hamilton, I had the unfortunate experience of losing $950 to a dishonest car salesman. Determined to seek justice, I obtained a lawyer and persisted all year to get my money returned so I could attend forestry college in January 1965.

It was a stressful time, but my persistence paid off and I was able to obtain justice in court. My money was returned in time for college.

A true determination and persistence story is told by Paul, a Canadian serving at a mission hospital in Nepal in 2013. He and his team were asked to build a nursing station for the medical ward of the hospital in the mission courtyard. The challenge was that a massive slab of granite rock at the proposed site limited any prospects for construction.

With much bravado and faith, Paul stated that he would remove the granite, even though all others believed it to be an impossible task. At the time, Paul actually had no idea how he would remove the rock, since diamond-drilling equipment was unavailable then, and it was discovered that picks and shovels weren't up to the task.

Paul asked his local man, Raju, how they would remove the rock. Wanting to help, Raju remembered the time when his father had told him a story about workers previously removing rocks from construction sites in Nepal. Since dynamite was unavailable, workers had placed used tires on bare rock, soaked them with fuel oil, and then kept a large and hot fire burning. A brief time later, the large rocks had split into small pieces, allowing the workers to gather up the broken stones.

Now inspired, Paul got out propane torches and tanks and directed the hot flames onto the rock. In just a few minutes, the rocks exploded and cracked into pieces. The workers eagerly gathered them up, broke them down further, and used them later for gravel fill.

For a month, the motivated team worked feverishly. The rock was soon fully removed and the nursing station was built.

Everyone thought the task of removing that granite would be impossible, but a challenge of a difficult nature gives rise to a person's creative juices. Through working together towards a common cause, this seemingly impossible task was accomplished through determination and persistence by people of faith to the glory of God.

8
BUILD SOLID RELATIONSHIPS WITH YOUR FAMILY AND COMMUNITY

AT MY THREE-unit apartment, one of my senior tenants had two married daughters who lived in British Columbia. They had urged their mother numerous times to relocate and move in with them so she could see more of her grandchildren. Although she appreciated her daughters' offers, she said, "I'm staying in Kapuskasing because my friends are here." She never did relocate.

A very practical piece of advice from the Bible is found in Romans 12:18: *"If it is possible, as far as it depends on you, live at peace with everyone."* It is always prudent not to burn your bridges or remain on bad terms with someone which could put you in an awkward position down the road. They just might be in a position to influence your future.

I am happy that for the most part I got along quite well with the people I've dealt with. After all, there are those with long memories who patiently wait for a payback opportunity to make up for a perceived wrong they may have endured through a decision you once made.

When my company downsized, some staff members found that they had to change departments while others were laid off.

The employees were actually given the opportunity to choose who they would prefer to work under. This was a prime example of management exercising the Golden Rule, and the value of doing so.

The Golden Rule is the principle of treating others as we ourselves would want to be treated. In the Bible, it's phrased this way: *"So in everything, do to others what you would have them do to you..."* (Matthew 7:12)

Just this week, I talked with a young man I worked with briefly before I retired in 2004. I needed a favour in regards to a site for snow deposit near his property. Because we'd had no disagreements, he was most happy to grant my request.

I got along well with most of my apartment tenants in my thirty-five years as a landlord. I dealt promptly with repairs and only infrequently increased their rents. One of the tenants told me that when you're a tenant at Mr. Lemon's apartment, you may stay for life.

Recently I listened to a radio interview with a beloved and respected doctor who was about to retire. A retirement party was organized for him by those doctors he had taught years before in medical school. This doctor had made it a rule to treat upcoming doctors with dignity and respect. He'd had the foresight to realize he might have a need for their medical expertise in the future if he required surgery. He had thought he would be more relaxed knowing that his emergency care would be handled by someone with whom he had good relations.

A number of years ago, a senior Christian widow from Sudbury was looking for an apartment in Kapuskasing. A landlord asked her for references, but she had none. When she said that she was friends with Warren and Evelyn Lemon, though, he said that was good enough for him. He accepted her as a tenant.

She told us this later, remarking that we obviously had a good reputation.

In 2021, I drove into a car wash. Upon backing out, the large garage door started to close on its own and smashed the rear window of my van. The owner was upset, claiming that I had backed into his garage door. This wasn't true. But rather than attempt to settle the matter in a small claims court, I absorbed the $450 replacement cost. I didn't want to have hard feelings with him and his family while living in the same town.

Three sisters in the Lord for fifty years.

My family in January 1966.

9

DISPLAY STRENGTH AND COURAGE

GOD PROMISED TO assist Joshua as he was about to lead the Israelite nation into the promised land. These promises can assist you also!

> No one will be able to stand against you all the days of your life. As I was with Moses, so I will be with you; I will never leave you nor forsake you. *Be strong and courageous*, because you will lead these people to inherit the land I swore to their ancestors to give them.
>
> *Be strong and very courageous.* Be careful to obey all the law my servant Moses gave you; do not turn from it to the right or to the left, that you may be successful wherever you go. Keep this Book of the Law always on your lips; meditate on it day and night, so that you may be careful to do everything written in it. Then you will be prosperous and successful. Have I not commanded you? *Be strong and courageous.* Do not be afraid; do not be discouraged, for

the Lord your God will be with you wherever
you go. (Joshua 1:5–9, emphasis added)

So be bold! When you reflect back on your life, you may regret more what you didn't do than what you did do. Sometimes a failure to act at the right moment is the biggest failure of all.

An anonymous writer once coined this phrase: "There is a choice you have to make in everything you do. So keep in mind that, in the end, the choice you make makes you."

An encouragement card supplied by Share Word Global. Those who send these cards make donations to the Gideons, helping the organization provide copies of God's Word throughout Canada and the world. Countless lives have been impacted by this work over the last century.

10
WHAT THE BIBLE SAYS ABOUT MONEY AND STEWARDSHIP

NEARLY FIFTEEN PERCENT of everything Jesus spoke about was related to money and possessions. Sixteen out of his fifty-two parables dealt with the topic of money. The only subject Jesus taught about more was the Kingdom of God.

In total, there are roughly 2,350 verses that concern money. This is about twice as many as there are about faith and prayer combined. The Scriptures are very clear about the connection between a person's spiritual life and their attitudes concerning money and possessions.

Even as a teen, I had the good common sense not to spend every dollar I earned. And I certainly felt reluctant to pay interest on my purchases. On my first job, I opened a registered retirement savings plan (RRSP) and saved $30.57 per month. This amount was deducted directly from my bank account so I never really missed it. It didn't first pass through my hands.

I kept increasing the amount until I reached the maximum. I invested in RRSPs until my retirement in 2004 at the age of sixty. I remember telling the young bank employees at my branch that I froze my RRSP account for five years in the 1980s and earned compound interest of six percent, eight percent, ten percent, and twelve percent. They were flabbergasted.

I have heard Dr. Charles Stanley state in sermons that he has a pretty good idea of many Christians' giving patterns. He has never known of a Christian in financial difficulty who has consistently and faithfully given of their tithes and offerings. Not one.

Another pastor stated that if you settle the matter of giving cheerfully and faithfully to the Lord's work, everything else will fall into its proper place.

Sadly, for some Christians, the last thing about them to get saved is their wallet!

Evelyn and I have tithed all of our lives. Never once have we held back, even when we were a bit short. Our tithe always came first. We also never used our giving as a weapon to get our own way on an issue.

I do know of some who have withheld their tithe because they were dissatisfied about something in the ministry. The Lord had to deal with them, and their spiritual life and legacy suffered because of their unwise choice.

The Lord promises,

> "Bring the whole tithe into the storehouse, that there may be food in my house. Test me in this," says the Lord Almighty, "and see if I will not throw open the floodgates of heaven and pour out so much blessing that there will not be room enough to store it." (Malachi 3:10)

Blessings can come in numerous ways: good health, a marriage free of strife, a godly family, and a productive and useful life free of harmful addictions, etc.

In 2010, I received a sizeable cheque from a totally unexpected source. In 2023, I received another cheque from a pension fund that I'd never dreamed of receiving additional funds from.

In 1997, I received a large amount from the sale of some company shares I had held for a few years. I invested some of these funds, modernized our home, helped our daughter in university, and gave to charity. I continue to reap benefits from that investment even today.

There once came a time when Evelyn quietly gave a sum of money to a needy Christian friend. In the following days, she unexpectedly earned twice that amount in her part-time job.

If a Christian shares with me that they're broke, I sense immediately that they aren't tithing. Therefore, they are being disobedient to God.

One of our neighbours once had to declare bankruptcy. In her own words, she had spent too freely and lived without a budget. Money had been no object to her.

Financial distress is just as much a source of marital breakdown for Christians as it is for unbelievers. A husband and wife must covenant together to control spending. If either one spends two dollars for every one dollar coming in, they will have constant strife. A couple can resolve to sacrifice now so they can party later, or they can party now and pay later—in their sunset years. Either way, they pay.

Most couples don't have an income problem; they have a spending problem.

Evelyn and I purchased a three-unit apartment in 1989 at the interest rate of 13.5 percent. Our goal was to pay it off as soon as possible so it could be a source of retirement income. Using every spare dollar, we paid for that unit by year twelve of the fifteen-year mortgage. This proved to be a wise investment.

The net income does assist in paying bills, allowing us to purchase the little extras in life without too much concern about cost. We do charge a lot of purchases, but we pay the amount in full before the credit card payment is due so as to keep interest costs at zero.

Because we've both been wise in our spending habits, living sensibly instead of buying every toy available, we are able to assist others in times of need.

In listening to input from a financial advisor, we once heard a recommendation to not hang out with big spenders. That could make you prone to overspending and upsetting your goals.

Evelyn and I assist in supporting this young family of five on the mission field.

11
CHRISTIAN CAMPING AND MISSION TRIPS

ENROLLING YOUR CHILDREN in a Christian camp, where they can be under twenty-four-hour Christian influence, will change their lives. And when they're older, if possible, take them personally to a mission field, even if only for one week.

In May 1967, I met the woman I would eventually marry at Camp Opasatica in Quebec. The camp so fired us up that we were determined to evangelize our hometowns as soon as we got back. Evelyn and I were engaged at Camp Opasatica in May 1969, the only couple to get engaged while attending that camp. We've been married fifty-five years as of August 2024.

At the 2013 Share Word Global convention in Prince Edward Island, a husband and wife shared about their missions trip to Vanuatu, a volcanic island in the south Pacific. A total of seven Canadians participated, including the couple's sixteen-year-old granddaughter, in Bible distribution and evangelism. An adventure like this will change a teen forever and bond the family more closely together. At the end, the granddaughter only had one question: "How old do I have to be before I can join the Gideons?"

At another Share Word Global convention in 2022, three teens from Woodland Christian High School in Guelph,

Ontario, along with their teacher, shared about their missions trip to Brazil in 2022. A total of thirty youth from Brazil and Canada joined together to share Jesus with the local population. The teens all said that their faith in Christ had been strengthened and that they would go again. They were so excited when they made their presentations![4]

As a young boy growing up in Chipman, New Brunswick, I attended a Christian camp called Camp Wegesegum. Numerous boys there had little or no religious upbringing, but a full day of religious teaching, activities, and influence has a positive effect on a child for the rest of their life. A lot of adults can trace their salvation moment back to their early camping experiences.

In our later years, Evelyn and I drove our own girls to a Christian camp, as well as some non-churched kids. The children were all a bit hesitant at first to be left for a week, but they were all smiles when we returned a week later to pick them up. They were exuberant and couldn't wait to go back the next year.

In September 2023, I left Kapuskasing in my van with three other Christian men, heading for a men's retreat at Silver Birches Camp in Kirkland Lake, Ontario. It was a four-hour drive, but we had a really great time of Christian fellowship on the trip.

Much of the blessings of any camp or mission experience come from just getting to know better those with whom you're travelling. There were one hundred men in total, of all ages and from different areas of Ontario. All had stories to tell. With that number, some were hurting for one reason or another and needed prayer, understanding, and healing. There was also time to settle in, enjoy wholesome food, fellowship, share, have fun, and relax. Most importantly, we heard sound, relevant biblical teaching from a speaker on issues that affect men in their lives.

---

[4] More details of these two mission trips can be seen on the Share Word Global website: www.sharewordglobal.com

Guidance for Life

The key verse is this one, from Acts:

> But you will receive power when the Holy Spirit comes on you; and you will be my witnesses in Jerusalem, and in all Judea and Samaria, and to the ends of the earth. (Acts 1:8)

Camp Opasatica campers on May 22, 1967 in Rouyn, Quebec. One hundred fifty teens and youth being impacted and guided in life by visionary Christian leaders.

12
SUDBURY VISIT OF CROSSES

WHILE VISITING IN Sudbury, Ontario in 2023, my wife and I took photos of the one hundred fifty white wooden crosses in the downtown core. Each cross has the name of an individual who died of an opioid overdose or addiction to painkilling drugs.

On a recent radio broadcast, I heard a news report about a city in Alberta with the highest number of drug deaths in the province. Every province, city, and town in Canada has similarly sad stories of drug overdosing.

Unintentional injuries are the leading cause of death among young people, but the second cause of deaths for Canadian men between the ages of fifteen and thirty-four is suicide.

Drugs will not fill the void in a person's heart; only Jesus can fill that need. It's shocking to learn that drugs of all kinds are killing so many of our youth and causing heartbreak to innumerable families. It challenges us as individual Christians, churches, and Christian organizations to do what we can *before* people enter that cycle of despair.

Governments and society must realize that people need to be changed from the inside and be more supportive of those who are achieving notable results in giving hope, meaning, and salvation to those who so desperately need it. The gospel needs to be preached: there is a way, other than drugs, to redeem broken lives. It is possible only through salvation in Jesus and a life lived for Him.

Rather than constantly injecting additional funds and resources into assisting those with dire needs, governments need to get at the root of the problem.

Abundant Life Church in Kapuskasing has had a youth director for years. The programs they've instituted are making a difference in young people's lives. On Thursdays, Fridays, and Sundays, upwards of forty-five youth attend church functions, and at times they travel to other towns and cities.

Kapuskasing churches, and indeed other churches in the north, are impressing on our youth the need to resist addictive drugs, or anything else that can harm them, and embrace Christianity. Schools need to reintroduce biblical principles and teach the harmful effects of making improper choices so students don't embark on a destructive lifestyle. They should invite former addicts into schools to address the entire student body to warn of the consequences.

> I have no greater joy than to hear that my children are walking in the truth. (3 John 4)
>
> A wise son heeds his father's instruction... (Proverbs 13:1)

The one hundred fifty Crosses for Change in Sudbury, Ontario.

13
WHEN MEDITATING ON A BIBLE PASSAGE

WHEN I HUNTED with my dad in my younger days, he taught me that it is much more productive to cover a small area of forest thoroughly, walking it slowly to observe for hidden or disguised signs of wildlife.

Any hunter who keeps his head down and covers the ground too quickly will miss what's right in plain sight. If wildlife is in an area, the signs will usually be visible; the observant hunter just has to recognize what's there for him to see and act upon it.

We can glean a similar lesson about reading the Bible. I've heard many Christians say that they read the Bible… but they miss what they've just read. Others take great pleasure in reading large portions of Scripture but don't understand it.

In the Bible, meditation involves pondering God's Word and deeply reflecting on its truth. When Mary, the mother of Jesus, was in Bethlehem, after she had given birth, it is written that she *"treasured up all these things and pondered them in her heart"* (Luke 2:19).

It is well known that the Holy Spirit speaks to Christians who read His Word. Sometimes the Word is clear and easily understood, such as when it tells us not to marry an unbeliever, to give our tithes and offerings to God's work, and to attend church faithfully. Other times, readers may have to dig a little deeper to discern what God is telling them.

Christians naturally want to learn God's direction and guidance when they read and study the Scriptures. For more clarity, they can read what authors have written on certain topics or check other portions of the Bible in order to compare one scripture with another.

Here are a few thoughts we might look for when reading the Bible:

- Is this portion of Scripture still relevant to readers today?
- Is this passage clearly calling on me to confess or repent of a particular sin or act of disobedience?
- Is there a promise here that I can benefit from?
- Is my life in harmony with the general thought of this passage?
- Is there a change I need to make in my life to be drawn closer to God?

Christians who have a heartfelt desire to live with God's favour and blessing will meditate on God's Word to guide them in their daily lives and live in a positive way.

> ...but whose delight is in the law of the Lord, and who meditate on his law day and night. (Psalm 1:2)

14
GIVE THANKS FOR THE HARD TIMES

EVERYBODY HAS A problem they wish they didn't have. The Apostle Paul had a thorn in his side which plagued him, Naaman had the dreaded disease of leprosy, Moses had a stutter, King David had family challenges, King Saul had an obedience problem, etc.

> Yet man is born to trouble as surely as sparks
> fly upward. (Job 5:7)

My own thorn in the flesh has been a lifelong stutter. With a lot of willpower and persistence, I have thrived. But life has been difficult on occasion—and embarrassing. I have learned to cope with my stutter and realize that most people, fluent or otherwise, get hung up on their speech at stressful times.

If life was always a walk in the park, we wouldn't grow. Those with speech impediments are forced outside their comfort zone every day, making them grow. When I observe the health issues, mental problems, and addictions that so many people struggle with, I consider myself quite fortunate to only have a mild speech impediment.

When I encounter others who have a speech impediment, I am happy to inform them that help is available. It actually costs very little for an individual to attend a facility for treatment, and it can reap lifetime rewards.

I encouraged a senior man from Kapuskasing to attend the Institute for Stuttering Treatment and Research in Edmonton, Alberta in 1993. He was the oldest client to ever seek treatment in their three-week program. Another younger man accompanied him as a companion, as he, too, had a stutter. I had attended the same intensive course earlier in 1992.

I met a young American couple in Moose Factory, Ontario in 2010 who was ministering to the Indigenous people in the James Bay area. They had no children and found living in the north to be a severe cultural shock with the long, cold winters. With a friend, I visited the couple and the woman shared that she had cried every day during their first winter. They were adjusting to the hard times and growing with it, though. It was mid-February in their second winter and she hadn't yet cried up to that point in time.

Many senior couples have endured challenges in years past but endured and been strengthened. If I was seeking counsel on a troubling issue, I would be more inclined to seek counsel from one who had gone through a similar experience and come through it successfully.

15

MAKE WISE CHOICES THAT WILL MAKE YOUR PARENTS PROUD

AS A SINGLE man of twenty-five, I left for a three-week tour of the Holy Land in the spring of 1969 with twenty-six others. I told my parents I would have something important to tell them when I returned to Canada. I had prayed to God that if I greatly missed Evelyn while I was gone, I would purchase a wedding ring in Jerusalem and propose to her when I returned. This was my "fleece" to God.

I did miss her, I did purchase a ring, and I did propose. My mom later told me that she had discerned I was either going to propose to Evelyn or declare my decision to attend a Bible college.

I have told a number of young men and women about how important it is to live their lives so as to please their parents, who have sacrificed so much for them.

In January 2020, I was with an eighteen-year-old single man, along with his mother and grandmother. I had just accepted him as a tenant and his mom and grandmother were happy that their son had a suitable place to live. In the presence of this man's family, I told him that his mother and grandmother obviously loved him very much, as they were willing to pay his first month's rent. I encouraged him to live his life so as to please his family and make them proud.

The two older women were happy that I had given this charge to their young family member.

Three years later, he left for a supervisory position in Sudbury. I told him how much I felt he had matured in that time, which made his family proud.

My sister Linda told me recently that she learned that one of our uncles on our mom's side believed that our parents had done a pretty good job of raising us three kids. Our uncle wasn't gifted when it came to expressing compliments, so Linda had thought this a positive endorsement.

In October 2023, Evelyn and I stopped at a coffee shop before going to church. A senior man whose wife had recently died sat down at our table to talk. His wife had been a Christian, but he wasn't interested in religion. I knew he wasn't interested in attending church that morning, but I looked him in the eye and invited him to join us. He looked at us as he got up to leave and said twice, "We need people like you."

I had mentioned to this man previously that he did his best to give off the impression of having a hardened heart. I further said, in love, that I had encountered many men whose hearts had been softened by Jesus—and Jesus could soften his heart also. He just shrugged it off.

In August 1973, I took my dad on a fly-in fishing trip to the west coast of Hudson's Bay. There were five men in total and we fished for brook trout on the Brant River, just ten miles south of Hudson's Bay. It was a memorable trip! I was glad I had arranged the trip, as Dad talked about it a lot to his friends and family when he returned to New Brunswick.

Later, in June and July of 1979, Dad and I embarked on a twenty-four-day holiday to British Columbia in his half-ton truck. We visited friends and relatives along the way and had a blessed time of bonding.

When in Banff, Alberta, he looked around at the stunning mountain scenery and said, "I wish my parents could have seen this country."

Upon returning home, Dad sent me a letter stating, in part, "And thanks very much for the holiday. Nicest vacation and grandest experience I ever had in my life."

Mom and Dad didn't attend our wedding in Timmins, Ontario on August 30, 1969. But they did send a letter to Evelyn's mother that said, "We know you miss Evelyn as much as we miss our three, but still they are safe in God's keeping. Warren describes Evelyn as a good Christian girl, which means a lot to him."

My wife has told me of another story in her life that illustrates how our choices can impact ourselves and others. When Evelyn was thirteen, she babysat at a home in Timmins. She noticed there was beer readily accessible to the children and mentioned this to the parents when they returned home. The mother stated that she would sooner see her children drink beer than consume sugary soft drinks. Evelyn's parents had broken up when she was five years old because her dad was an alcoholic. Evelyn had enough discernment and wisdom to reply that she had never heard of a family being broken up because they consumed soft drinks.

16
A TWELVE-POINT EXHORTATION FOR ALL

A KEY PORTION of the Bible for all can be found in Proverbs 3:1–12:

> My son, do not forget my teaching, but keep my commands in your heart, for they will prolong your life many years and bring you peace and prosperity.
>
> Let love and faithfulness never leave you; bind them around your neck, write them on the tablet of your heart. Then you will win favor and a good name in the sight of God and man.
>
> Trust in the Lord with all your heart and lean not on your own understanding; in all your ways submit to him, and he will make your paths straight.
>
> Do not be wise in your own eyes; fear the Lord and shun evil. This will bring health to your body and nourishment to your bones.
>
> Honor the Lord with your wealth, with the firstfruits of all your crops; then your barns

will be filled to overflowing, and your vats will brim over with new wine.

My son, do not despise the Lord's discipline, and do not resent his rebuke, because the Lord disciplines those he loves, as a father the son he delights in.

17

CREATE OR DO SOMETHING THAT WILL BE OF LASTING VALUE TO YOURSELF AND OTHERS

I HAVE READ at least ten times *When God Builds a Church* by Bob Russell. One sentence speaks out to me on faith: "Instead of scoffing at the crazy ideas of the visionaries around you, seek their advice and listen wisely. God may be trying to lead you."[5]

In his concluding paragraph, the author challenges his readers:

> Put your hope in a big God who can fulfill big dreams. Determine you will try something so big that if God isn't in it, you will fail. Ask God to give you a vision that you should set out to do.[6]

I once read a story in the *Power for Living* Sunday school paper, dated December 21, 2003. The story was about the Christmas carol "Joy to the World." Isaac Watts (1674–1748) composed this carol at the inspiration of Scripture.

---

[5] Bob Russell, *When God Builds a Church: Ten Principles for Growing a Dynamic Church* (West Monroe, LA: Howard Publishing, 2000), 135.
[6] Ibid., 277.

Young Isaac wasn't at all happy with the hymns of the day in England. He expressed his displeasure on many occasions to his exasperated father, to which his father replied, "If you don't like the hymns we sing, then write better ones."

Seventeen-year-old Isaac did just that and wrote new hymns for 226 consecutive weeks. He was ordained as a pastor in 1695 at the age of twenty-one and became known as the father of English melody. "Joy to the World" is perhaps the most joyous, triumphant Christmas hymn ever written.

I have given away or placed thousands of copies of Gideon Bibles in my nearly fifty years with that ministry. I've visited a host of schools and classrooms to present a free New Testament to eager youth and emphasize the importance of reading and caring for the most valuable book they will ever own. I always leave them with this verse: *"I have hidden your word in my heart that I might not sin against you"* (Psalm 119:11).

In April 1990, I embarked on a twelve-day Gideon distribution and evangelism journey to Venezuela. Together with thirty other Gideons from six countries, we placed or distributed 615,000 copies of Scriptures. God impacted countless lives for Christ on that trip. Only time will tell how many lives have been saved because of our obedience to distribute God's Word nationally and internationally.

Evelyn and I have distributed Bibles in Toronto and Vancouver. We've met a host of godly men and women in our ministry and travels. Their lives have left a lasting impression on ours and we trust that we have been a blessing to them as well.

Along with others, we have also made a meaningful contribution to the lives of the numerous youth we've had the privilege of hosting in our homes. Some are now pastors, missionaries, or Christian workers. We know that these combined ministries have influenced many people in the present. They have told us so.

Spirit-filled Christians are equipped to recognize and respond to people's obvious needs and misery. This is the result of sin, the power of Satan, and making poor choices in life.

I am also a prayer and financial supporter of a local Christian radio station. Because of this, my wife and I were both given light jackets that state on the back, "Hope Changes Everything." I wear it every day when the weather is favourable.

When three other men and I were distributing Gideon New Testaments to students on the James Bay coast, we told every classroom that we were dealers in hope. Then we related what we meant, for we are supposed to encourage and give the bread of life to hungry souls. Our challenge is to be creative in getting the Word out so people will come to Christ long after we have gone.

My present goal in life is simple: "Don't mess up." I wouldn't want to undo in a moment what God has enabled Evelyn and me to do in our many years of Christian service together.

I took my marriage vows seriously and never had to tell my wife that I was unfaithful to her or to my two daughters. When our younger daughter was in Kindergarten, she noticed that some of her classmates revealed their distress about their parents separating. She became concerned and asked Evelyn if she and I would ever separate as parents. Evelyn assured both of our daughters that we would be staying together.

The greatest legacy of lasting value that parents can pass on to their children is their Christian legacy.

In August 2010, Dr. J. Kent Edwards spoke at a Gideon convention in Calgary, delivering a message on leadership, decisions, and personal impact. He asked two questions in particular. Will my decisions glorify God and advance God's kingdom? Will my decisions help others to glorify God? If the answer to either question is no, then don't do it. It's not of

God. Seek older and younger counsel. The decisions you make will determine your impact in life.

Have you heard the account of an American businessman who invested in gold and pharmaceuticals in Timmins, Ontario in the early 1900s? Frederick Schumacher obviously impacted the town, as a suburb of Timmins has since been named in his honour.

Starting in 1916, Schumacher donated a Christmas toy to every child living in that suburb on a yearly basis.

Although he died in Iowa in 1957, his descendants still draw funds from a foundation each year to continue the tradition of these children's gifts. In 2023, gifts were given to one hundred seventy-three children. For the past thirty years, the sum of $7,000 is given for volunteer firemen to purchase toys and distribute them. Each gift contains the name of the recipient along with a picture of Mr. Schumacher.

This man is spoken of with great affection by children and parents. His legacy has carried on every year since 1916. I don't know if Mr. Schumacher was a Christian, but it's easy to visualize the lasting impact his kind contribution would have if there was a Christian message included along with the gifts.

When it comes to leaving a lasting legacy, the name of John Bunyan should come to mind. He lived from 1628 to 1688. His parents weren't always a good example and young Bunyan was considered to be a "ringleader in wickedness."[7] He wrote,

> It was my delight to be taken captive by the devil at his will. I had few equals with my cursing, lying, and blaspheming the holy name of God.[8]

---

[7] *A Pilgrim's Progress: The Story of John Bunyan* (London, UK: Ambassador Films, 2010), DVD. Narrated by Derick Bingham.
[8] Ibid.

God protected and preserved John and the Holy Spirit convicted him of his sin. Devout Christians of the day also influenced John's life greatly; a pastor saw potential in John, became his mentor, and led him to Christ.

Bunyan wrote forty books, the most influential being *The Pilgrim's Progress*, an allegorical story. This simple tinker of Bedford, the immortal dreamer, has influenced more lives than most men. Even today, three hundred fifty years after it was written, *The Pilgrim's Progress* outsells every other book except the Bible.

Most of us won't be as blessed as John Bunyan to leave such a lasting legacy, but we can all leave something of lasting value to others.

ABOUT THE AUTHOR

WARREN LEMON WAS born on January 1, 1944 in Chipman, New Brunswick. He has an older brother and a younger sister. His father owned two trucks. His dad hauled logs for the local sawmill, clay for a brick plant, and in later years was a bulk oil and gas distributor. His mother was a devoted and loving housewife who was always there for her family.

Warren moved to Hamilton, Ontario at the age of nineteen after graduating from Chipman Regional High School in 1963 with forty-three others. He worked at a steel mill in Hamilton from 1963–1964, after which he was accepted in 1965 to attend the Ontario Forest Ranger school near Huntsville. On January 5, 1966, Warren started a nearly forty-year career in the Woodlands Division of the Spruce Falls Power and Paper Company in Kapuskasing, Ontario.

He married Evelyn Dunbrack in August 1969 in Timmins. Together they raised two daughters, Audrey and Janice. Warren and Evelyn are equally yoked spiritually and have served God together in their church in Kapuskasing and in Share Word Global (the Gideons).

Warren wrote his first book, *Impacting Lives*, in November 2021 at the age of seventy-seven. In that book, he related how the lives of those in the past can leave a positive legacy for future generations. In 2024, he wrote this book for Christian youth and adults, although it contains useful instruction for those in all walks and stages of life.

Warren can be reached at ewlemon@live.com.

www.ingramcontent.com/pod-product-compliance
Lightning Source LLC
Chambersburg PA
CBHW061249040426
42444CB00010B/2324